AF610784

Alleged Pirate

The Legend of Captain John Sinclair of Smithfield and Gloucester, Virginia

BY
Thomas T. Wiatt

Published by Lulu Publishing & Limelight Publishing.

Copyright © 2022 Thomas T. Wiatt

All Rights Reserved.

No part of this publication may be reproduced, stored in a retrieval system, or transmitted in any form, or by any means; electronic, mechanical, photocopying, recording, or otherwise, without prior written permission from the copyright owner and publisher.

ISBN: 978-1-4717-5503-3

lulu.com

limelightpublishing.com

Come, brave boys, and fill your glasses,
You have humbled one proud foe,
No brave action this surpasses;
Fame shall tell the nations so -
Thus, be Britain's, woes completed,
Thus, abridged her cruel reign,
Till she, ever thus defeated,
Yields the scepter of the main,

Philip Freneau 1778

Acknowledgements

I would like to acknowledge the writers who came before me, those who took a deep interest in Captain Sinclair and put his story to the page. These include fellow descendants as Jefferson Sinclair Selden, Jr., Caroline Baytop Sinclair, and Barbara J. Allmand. Most of all I would like to acknowledge Claude O. Lanciano, Jr. who owned and lived in Captain Sinclair's home of Lands' End for many years and who wrote so much about the Captain. All these people helped provide much of the source material for this book.

Also, I would like to thank the Mariners' Museum in Newport News, Virginia for many of the photographs and giving me access to their amazing nautical library. The image on the front cover is courtesy of United Empire Miniatures. The image on the back cover is courtesy of Osprey Bloomsburg Publishing. A great deal of thanks goes to Chris Basford, Herb Greene and Laura Beavers for their amazing editing skills.

Foreword

Captain John Sinclair was a hero of the American Revolution and also my fourth great grandfather. I knew nothing about him until 1964 when a distant cousin of mine wrote a book entitled, *The Sinclair Family of Virginia*. I was thirteen when I acquired this book from my grandfather, Todd Wiatt, whose own mother was Maude Sinclair, the great-grand daughter of the Captain himself. From this book, and through family stories, I was intrigued by the tales of Captain John Sinclair whom some say may have been a pirate. What American teenage boy would not be fascinated by the idea that buccaneer blood might flow through his veins?

Since no one ever bothered to paint or even sketch a portrait of the captain while he was living and since he lived long before the invention of photography, there are no known images of John Sinclair. The image on the cover is used only to represent Captain John Sinclair. The silhouettes of some of the Sinclair family members are also used only to represent them but are based on some family facial characteristics.

There are also no known illustrations of any of the ships that Captain Sinclair owned or commanded. The photographs of the model ships on these pages are of similar design to Sinclair's ships and are used only to represent them.

-Thomas T. Wiatt 2020

Contents

Illustrations

INTRODUCTION

People such as George Washington, Thomas Jefferson, John Adams, Alexander Hamilton and Benjamin Franklin did not know John Sinclair personally, but they certainly knew of him. He was also known to the Virginia governors Patrick Henry, Henry Lee and Robert Brooke. A list of his acquaintances would include the likes of Lafayette, Comte de Grasse, John Marshall, and perhaps John Paul Jones.

Today, what is known about Captain John Sinclair is that he was a naval hero of the American Revolutionary War. During the war, he was a successful privateer and blockade runner, activities that brought much needed supplies for the American cause. In peace time he returned to his career as a merchant seaman, farmer and family man. He enjoyed the respect, esteem and love of the people in his hometown of Smithfield, Virginia. In 1795 he found himself in the courthouse in Williamsburg, Virginia being tried for piracy.

It is sometimes difficult to separate history from legend, or fact from fiction. The past, being gone, makes it difficult to know exactly what happened. All we have are documents, sometimes written by well-meaning people who had access to false information or people with their own agendas who may have embellished the truth.

Nearly all the information that is known about Captain John Sinclair started with tales told by his daughter-in-law to her grandchildren. Some of those grandchildren told the tales to their own grandchildren, many of whom wrote them down. We also have facts that are well documented, court records and eye-witness accounts.

This biography attempts to paint a portrait of a sometimes bitter and stubborn man of many idiosyncrasies. He was a man who was used to having his own way and being obeyed. He was the captain and master of many ships, but often not of his own family.

Through much research, this book attempts to separate fact from fiction. The author has taken some liberties in the portrayal of John Sinclair's innermost thoughts and emotions.

An Attempt at a Definition

The line between pirate and privateer has been a fine one throughout history, but never more so than during the period of the American Revolution. A "Letter of Marque" was the official commission issued by a sovereign government authorizing attacks on merchant vessels with which that government was at war. The fact that Britain did not recognize the American government made the line between pirate and privateer even finer.

The American privateers played a larger part in winning the Revolutionary War than has been generally recognized. Stung by their exploits, the fact was clearly perceived by Englishmen of that period. Although American privateers rarely menaced British naval vessels, their widespread attacks against British commerce was a constant source of harassment and humiliation.

Privateering during the American revolt for independence has been labeled one of the chief American industries because of the importance it assumed in making foreign products, and especially contraband available to the war effort.

When legal, privateering was considered a gentleman-like profession for the officers as it entailed no heavy work. The less physical labor a man had to do in the colonial period, the higher was his social status. In that day privateering was regarded as patriotic, fashionable, and enterprising. Captain John Sinclair was no doubt a privateer, but after the war, he may have crossed that line to pirate or at least helped pirates by outfitting and arming their ships. This author will let the reader be the judge.

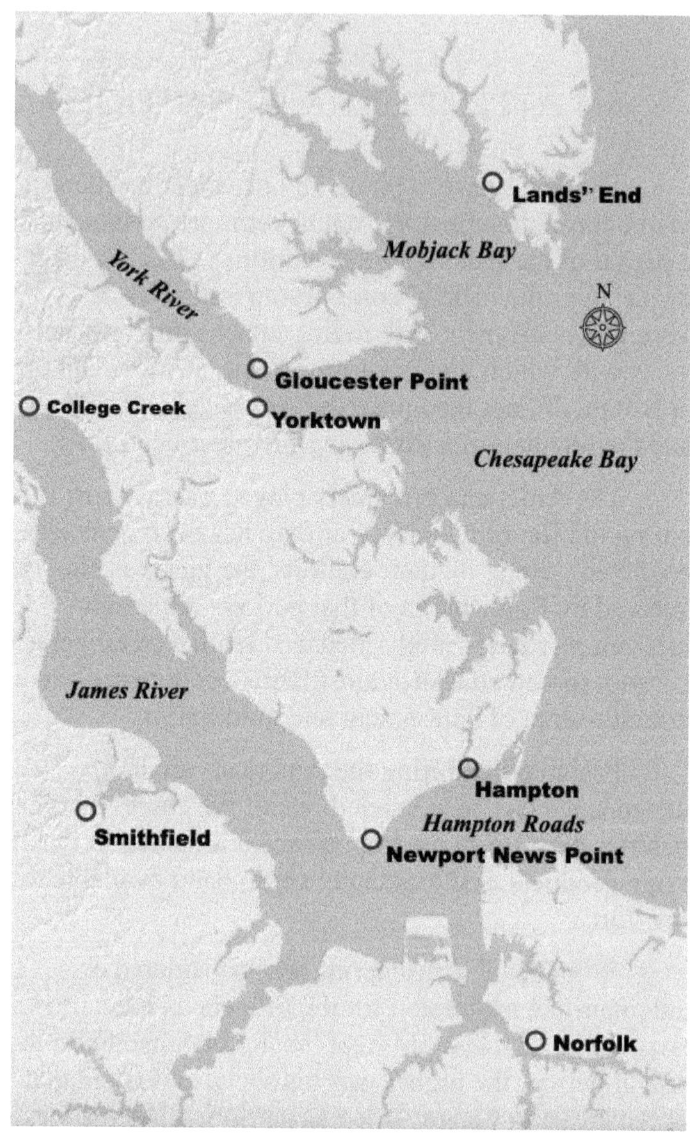

Hampton Roads, Virginia 1775

CHAPTER ONE

Family Background (1734)

There is a history in all men's lives

– William Shakespeare 1597

John Sinclair was the son of a Scottish immigrant named James Henry Sinclair. The circumstance of Henry Sinclair's coming to America in 1734 was an unusual one: he did not come voluntarily. He was kidnapped from his home in Aberdeen, Scotland and forcibly brought to the shores of America.

In the early eighteenth century, Scotland was a dangerous place. Wars, crime and corruption ran rampant throughout the country. The practice of kidnapping young Scottish boys and selling them as indentured servants was commonplace in the 1730's. This practice was especially bad in the port city of Aberdeen, Scotland.

An estimated 1,000 of Aberdeen's young boys met their fate this way during the period from 1730 to 1750. These were times when gangs roamed the streets of Aberdeen seizing young boys and selling them to merchant seamen who in turn would take them to the Americas to be sold as indentured servants. Even the Aberdeen government officials were paid off to look the other way. So flagrant was the practice that people, in the countryside near Aberdeen, avoided bringing children into the city for fear that they might be stolen. Wealth or status offered no immunity to the practice of kidnapping. This is what happened to five-year-old James Henry Sinclair, great-nephew of Alexander Sinclair, the 9th Earl of Caithness, Scotland.

The Sinclairs were from an ancient Scottish family whose name was originally Saint Clair and of Norman-French origin. They are descendants of Prince Henry Saint Clair (c. 1345 - c. 1400) the Scottish explorer, and for many centuries, the Sinclairs were the traditional Earls of Caithness, Scotland. James Henry Sinclair was born in Aberdeen, Scotland in 1729. Henry's father was Donald Sinclair and although the grandson of the Earl of Caithness, Donald had an older brother so it was thought that he would probably not inherit the title.

Donald Sinclair is said to have had some kind of dispute with a Virginia merchant seaman by the name of Captain Meredith. Captain Meredith was engaged in ocean trade between Britain and its American Colonies. The dispute was believed to be over some shipping matter and probably some large sum of money was involved. It was certain that it was Captain Meredith who kidnapped young Henry (as he was called), but his reasons may never be known. Perhaps it was to extract a ransom or just for some sort of revenge. The Captain never returned Henry, so a kidnapping for ransom does not seem likely. It is more likely it was because of a policy called headrights. The headrights system was introduced in Colonial America as a means to solve the labor shortage. Colonists could be granted an extra fifty acres of land for each worker they brought with them regardless of age. Since Captain Meridith had settled in Virginia and raised Henry as his own son, the headrights policy is a plausible reason for the kidnapping.

Some believe that Henry had a nurse who may have been involved in setting up the taking of five-year-old

Henry. Perhaps the nurse agreed to help in order to gain passage to America on Captain Meredith's ship. For whatever reason, Captain Meridith sailed away to Hampton, Virginia with young Henry. The boy was never to see his family again.

They disembarked at Fort George (now called Fort Monroe) then to the Captain's modest home on Queen Street in what is now downtown Hampton. Captain Meredith had become very fond of the child and decided to adopt him as his own. Strangely, the Captain elected to have Henry Sinclair keep his own name. Perhaps Captain Meredith wanted to keep open the possibility of collecting a ransom for the boy in case he changed his mind about Henry.

Apparently, he did not change his mind because Captain Meredith raised Henry and taught him the ways of the sea. By 1744, at only fifteen years of age, Henry became the cabin boy on his adopted father's ship. A few years later, as a young man, Henry came to own his own ship and was very much engaged in the commerce of Virginia. He settled in Smithfield, Virginia and was married in 1750 to Martha Brock of Sherwood, Gloucester County, Virginia. They had three children: John, Thomas and Mary.

In 1768 a lawyer from Scotland appeared in New York trying to locate Henry Sinclair. He placed messages in journals throughout the colonies stating that he was looking for a James Henry Sinclair of Aberdeen, Scotland. Henry responded to this message soon after it was brought to his attention and made arrangements to meet with the lawyer.

The lawyer carried with him news that Henry's uncle and father were dead, and he was now the rightful Earl of Caithness if only he would return to Scotland. Henry Sinclair refused the offer. He is said to have stated something to the effect that he did not believe in aristocracy, or the power which comes by inheritance. He said that he was a Virginian now and believed that every man should make his own way.

James Henry Sinclair often visited Aberdeen, Scotland in his capacity as a merchant seaman, but never tried to locate any of his relatives there. He died in 1790, having lived long enough to see his son, John Sinclair, become a hero in the American Revolutionary War.

Ship Model of an 18th Century Sloop Representing *The Andrew*
The Mariners' Museum and Park, Newport News, Virginia.

Chapter Two

The Seaman (1755)

The voice of the sea speaks to the soul

- Kate Chopin 1899

John Sinclair was born probably in the small port town of Hampton, Virginia in 1755. Today Hampton is a city on the Chesapeake Bay that boasts about being the oldest continuous English-speaking community in America. It was founded in 1610 on the remains of the Kecoughtan Indians' village shortly after the English forced the Indians to relocate. The city also has the dubious distinction of being the site of the first arrival of African Slaves in British North America.

By the time of John's birth, Hampton was incorporated as a town under Virginia law and was a thriving seaport. In order to control trade and collect duties, the English designated eight Virginia towns as ports and Hampton was one of those towns.

John Sinclair certainly grew up surrounded by a nautical way of life and was most likely trained by his father, Henry Sinclair, in the ways of the sea. His father was a very successful merchant seaman in Hampton, Virginia. While John's father was a very successful merchant seaman, little is known of his mother. John served on many of his father's ships as a mate and became familiar with many foreign ports, including those of Europe and the West Indies.

Although no images of John exist, he was described as being tall (about six feet) and lean with dark hair and blue eyes. He was stubborn and was used to getting his way. It is believed that John did not receive any formal education, although the community of Hampton had public schools that dated back to 1647. He would certainly have to know a great deal of mathematics in order to be able to navigate a ship. John was also fluent in French, perhaps out of necessity because of trading with French colonies of the West Indies.

John was also known to have a quick temper. Even when his temper was controlled, his anger could be felt by all those around him. He was quick to take offense and might be irritated over even the most minor matters. Forgiveness, nor the ability to forget, were not considered to be his strong points.

Probably around the mid 1770's John Sinclair moved from Hampton to the nearby town of Smithfield, Virginia, a part of Isle of Wight County. The town of Smithfield is located on the Pagan River which flows into the James River and then into the Chesapeake Bay. The Pagan River was named from the Algonquin Indian language word for pecan.

Smithfield was established as a seaport and an official tobacco inspection station at that time. The town was founded in 1634 and has not drastically changed since John Sinclair walked its cobblestone streets. Today Smithfield is still a quaint town filled with colonial-era architecture.

As a citizen of Smithfield, nineteen-year-old John was able to acquire his own ship around 1774, a small sloop named *The St. Andrew* and he became its master. Sloops were generally smaller than schooners and had the advantage of requiring fewer crew members.

The St. Andrew had one triangular mainsail and one headsail arranged longitudinally and with its fixed keel was more suitable for shallow waters along the coastal regions of Virginia and Maryland. Her speed and maneuverability made it easier to navigate the shoals of the coast and to hide in remote coves if need be.

Sinclair's best friend, John Pasteur, became his first mate on *The St. Andrew*. From 1774 to 1776 they engaged in a profitable trade in Indigo and coffee with Bermuda as well as St. Eustacia and St. Kitts in the West Indies.

Sinclair and Pasteur were good friends on both land and sea. They lived near each other on Church Street in Smithfield. As sailors often do, they shared many adventures together in ports up and down the east coast, except for the port of Smithfield, Virginia. They were, what we would call today drinking buddies, but a woman came between them.

John Pasteur had been keeping company with a young lady named Elizabeth Anne Wilson who lived near Smithfield, and while in that port all his time was spent with her. Captain Sinclair knew her family and was quite taken by her charms as well.

John Sinclair actually asked John Pasteur's permission to also could court Anne (as she was called), in sort of an open competition. Strangely, Pasteur agreed, but this did not work out well for him and Anne chose the Captain over the first mate.

John Pasteur showed no open disdain, but left Sinclair's employment shortly thereafter. Pasteur became the Captain of his own sloop, *The Molly* in 1776. *The Molly* was a small schooner with a twenty-five-ton capacity, carried arms and required a four-man crew. John Pasteur's loss was later compensated for when he married Anne's younger sister, Honour Wilson, in 1782.

Captain John Sinclair and Anne Wilson became Captain and Mrs. John Sinclair on October 3, 1774. Despite the turbulent years of the American Revolution, the couple bore and raised five children. Like many people in America, Sinclair saw the war coming and was prepared.

Ship Model of an 18th Century Schooner Representing
The Molly
The Mariners' Museum and Park, Newport News, Virginia.

IN CONGRESS.

The DELEGATES of the UNITED COLONIES of *New-Hampſhire*, *Maſſachuſetts-Bay*, *Rhode-Iſland*, *Connecticut*, *New-York*, *New-Jerſey*, *Pennſylvania*, the Counties of *New-Caſtle*, *Kent* and *Suſſex* on *Delaware*, *Maryland*, *Virginia*, *North-Carolina*, *South-Carolina*, and *Georgia*, TO All unto whom theſe Preſents ſhall come, ſend GREETING: KNOW YE,

THAT we have granted, and by theſe Preſents do grant Licence and Authority to *John Sinclair* Mariner, Commander of the *schooner* called Nicholson of the Burthen of *thirty* Tons, or thereabouts, belonging to *John Sinclair* of Smithfield in the Colony of Virginia mounting *eight* Carriage Guns, and navigated by *twenty* Men, to fit out and ſet forth the ſaid *schooner* in a warlike Manner, and by and with the ſaid *schooner* Nicholson and the Crew thereof, by Force of Arms, to attack, ſeize, and take the Ships and other Veſſels belonging to the Inhabitants of Great-Britain, or any of them, with their Tackle, Apparel, Furniture and Ladings, on the High Seas, or between high-water and low-water Marks, and to bring the ſame to ſome convenient Ports in the ſaid Colonies, in Order that the Courts, which are or ſhall be there appointed to hear and determine Cauſes civil and maritime, may proceed in due Form to condemn the ſaid Captures, if they be adjudged lawful Prize; the ſaid *John Sinclair* having given Bond, with ſufficient Sureties, that Nothing be done by the ſaid *schooner* or any of the Officers, Mariners or Company thereof contrary to, or inconſiſtent with the Uſages and Cuſtoms of Nations, and the Inſtructions, a Copy of which is herewith delivered to him. And we will and require all our Officers whatſoever to give Succour and Aſſiſtance to the ſaid *John Sinclair* in the Premiſes. This Commiſſion ſhall continue in Force until the Congreſs ſhall iſſue Orders to the Contrary.

By Order of the Congreſs,

Dated at Norfolk
the 5th of October 1776

John Hancock PRESIDENT.

A Reproduction of John Sinclair's Letter of Marque

Chapter Three

The Privateer (1776)

One man's pirate is another man's Privateer.

– Captain Henry Morgan 1688

By the spring of 1774, the relationship between England's colonies and the mother country were deteriorating rapidly. The British were determined to raise revenue at the expense of the colonies to pay for the French and Indian War (the Seven Years War). Attempts to raise revenue through the Stamp Act were considered particularly imposing, especially in port towns like Hampton and Smithfield. Sea going trade generated numerous transactions that were subject to this unpopular tax.

To add insult to injury, American seamen were offended by the disparaging remarks aimed in their direction made by their British counterparts. The British in general looked down on the "colonials" and thought them crude and somewhat uncivilized.

Many citizens of the Commonwealth carried strong anti-British feelings but the folks who lived along the James River and Hampton Roads had more than most. Captain Sinclair's anti-British feelings were considered extreme, even by local standards. His hatred for anything British was probably forged early in life.

By early 1775, Britain's relations with its American colonies had further deteriorated and most American Seamen supported the rebels by boycotting English goods.

After the first shots were fired near Lexington and Concord, Massachusetts in April 1775, the British imposed an embargo against all commerce. When Britain's King George III issued the "Proclamation of Rebellion" in August 1775, the embargo was expanded into a general blockade, with the objective of stopping all commerce that might help the rebel cause. This blockade, of course, only intensified Sinclair's hatred of the British.

One of Virginia's first armed conflicts of the American Revolution took place in Hampton. The crew of a British sloop named *H.M.S. Otter* had been raiding Hampton and the surrounding for supplies. In September 1775, a storm forced the *Otter* to take refuge in the Hampton River, probably near the present-day Hampton Marina. The townspeople promptly seized the ship's cannons and set fire to some of the ship's supplies. In retribution, on October 24, 1775, the *Otter* returned and fired on the town of Hampton with its heavy guns. The local people of Hampton responded with such accurate gunfire that the British ship withdrew.

Late in 1775, the Congress authorized privateering and issued Letters of Marque to those who wished to help the war effort in that manner. This practice, legal piracy, not only hindered the enemy, but was also very profitable for ship owners since they retained a portion of the prize, usually about half. The ships needed to be fast and maneuverable to overcome the enemy. Since the privateering vessels carried no cargo, they were naturally quick. They sometimes disguised themselves as innocent fishing vessels, flying the flag of a neutral country and with their guns hidden until the last minute. When the time was right, they ran up their true flag and captured the enemy ship. A crew was then placed aboard the captured vessel and it was sailed to the nearest friendly port. After the court verified the Letter of Marque, the prize would be liquidated at auction and the money divided appropriately. The crew also received a portion. John Sinclair had such a hatred for the British that he found this very exciting as well as profitable.

Although the American colonies had yet to declare their independence, many of the colonies began to establish navies. In the spring of 1776, The Commonwealth of Virginia appointed a board of Naval Commissions to help raise a navy and acquire ships to help with the American rebel cause. John Sinclair became a Captain in the Virginia Navy and placed his sloop, *The St. Andrew,* into service for the American rebel cause. Records from September 1776 show that Captain Sinclair owned three other sloops in addition to *The St. Andrew* and all were placed in service to the American cause though skippered by other officers. Sinclair's ships were small and could almost be called large boats rather than ships. They were, however, capable of ocean passage and could outmaneuver the much larger British ships.

For several months thereafter, while aboard *The St. Andrew,* Sinclair smuggled arms and ammunition from the West Indies to the colonial forces. He was able to acquire a great fortune due to his sailing and smuggling abilities.

Even though, *The St. Andrew* was quick enough to slip through the British blockade, she was no match against a British warship in an armed conflict. The ship had to be able to avoid any of the British ships that were a part of the blockade. Captain Sinclair and his ship were very successful at this.

Captain Sinclair was soon to advance from smuggler to privateer. On the 5th of October 1776, he officially received the license and authority (or Letter of Marque) from the Congress of the United Colonies, signed by John Hancock, to attack by force of arms or to seize any ship belonging to the inhabitants of Great Britain. He had risen in status from a smuggler to a privateer. About this time Sinclair's old friend and sometimes rival, John Pasteur, also became a privateer with Sinclair's ship *The Molly.*

By early 1777, Captain Sinclair had sold his ship *The St. Andrew* and purchased a fine ship named *The Nicholson* and turned it over to the Virginia Navy while continuing as her commander. *The Nicholson* was a small two-mast schooner. She was armed and fast, but no match against the British warships. Captain Sinclair knew this and stuck to raiding small British merchant ships.

Schooners were usually a bit larger than sloops and an American innovation. Though they fared poorly for catching winds for long trans-Atlantic journeys they made up for that in their maneuverability and speed. With their larger size, schooners could be more heavily armed for a confrontation with a British ship.

In the beginning of the conflict, the British merchant ships were unarmed. This would change as the conflict escalated. Captain Sinclair, however, was willing to risk naval gunfire, along with stormy seas for the rewards that came with capturing a British vessel. He accomplished this with consistent success.

In the spring of 1777, the commercial trading vessels which had been under the Virginia Navy Board were placed under the Continental Army. William Aylette, a quartermaster general from Williamsburg, Virginia was placed in charge of these trading vessels. In April 1777 Aylette sent Captain Sinclair to St. Eustacia in the West Indies with a cargo of indigo. He returned with a cargo from a captured British merchant ship. A St. Eustacia merchant, Van Bibber, wrote to William Aylette of Captain Sinclair's exploits on April 10, 1777:

> The little boat *Nicholson*, Captain John Saintclare (sic) indicating her arrival the day preceding with an inbound shipment of 13 casks of idigo (sic)

> On April 21, 1777 Van Bibber wrote a second report:

> There just arrived here the Captain and crew of a fine schooner that sailed from here about two hours before [with] Captain Saintclare (sic) and was bound for Newfoundland but Captain Saint Clare (sic)....altered the schooners voyage to Virginia [actually Maryland] and landed much of his crew (as did not choose to go to Virginia) on the Island of Saba [Dutch West Indies]. I am told Captain Sinclaires (sic) Prize has on board 800 Joes in Specie 100 hhds of Rum & 24 Sugar...He [Sinclair] appears to me to be the most deserving clever young fellow that I have seen...pardon me for entertaining you with my remarks and opinions of your officers.

This capture was confirmed by the May 9th edition of *The Virginia Gazette* newspaper stating the prize was taken to North Carolina and reported Captain Sinclair's safe arrival home.

The Virginia Gazette of May 19th also remarked upon the Captain's arrival noting that his ship brought back small arms, dry goods, etc., originating in France.

The Gazette went on to state that accompanying Captain Sinclair was a passenger identified only as a gentleman who had spent years in London and returned by way of the islands, carrying diplomatic dispatches to the U.S. Congress from the American "Ambassador from the Court of France." The article continues on about the "capture of the English schooner, recites her cargo and mentions that Captain Sinclair had directed her into a North Carolina port. The account quotes Sinclair as presuming her safe arrival if fair winds were met after he parted with her off the North Carolina coast.

The second notice containing a repetitious accounting of the captured cargo varies some from the first two reports. Its interest is in the mentioning of The Nicholson by name (but misspelled Nicolas) as an armed vessel belonging to Virginia.

This event was also mentioned in *The Maryland Gazette* newspaper a few weeks later.

> A small Virginia boat commanded by Capt. Sinclair (of Virginia) arrived here [Baltimore] the 16th…from South Carolina, with indigo. The 18th she sailed again, and that evening took a schooner with one hundred hogheads of rum, some sugars and 800 joes.

There are no detailed accounts of Captain Sinclair's methods, but actually boarding a British ship and close-up fighting were rare in Revolutionary War privateering. In most cases the British ship put up only a token resistance (if they resisted at all). Sinclair's ship usually would fire off a few cannon volleys perhaps causing a few casualties and the British merchant ship would surrender before any boarding was necessary. Sometimes, boarding would follow a gunnery engagement using the ship's broadside, and the defending ship's crew would be too disorganized and dazed by the cannon fire to put up much of a fight.

One of the tales known to have been handed down through the generations about Captain Sinclair is about a trip that *The Molly* made to Havana, Cuba for a shipload of greatly needed gun powder and ammunition. John Sinclair's friend John Pasteur had commanded the sloop, but in 1779 Captain Sinclair himself took command of the vessel. *The Molly* slipped through the British blockade in the James River without difficulty on her outbound voyage but during the ship's return with the precious cargo she had a very close call. Night had fallen by the time they were back in the James River; *The Molly* was halted by a British cruiser that inquired of her identity. It was said that Captain Sinclair coolly replied that his ship was a British supply ship. The Captain of the British cruiser did not call his bluff and *The Molly* was allowed to proceed unsearched.

Captain Sinclair then maneuvered his swift vessel through the inner patrol to bring her safely to his inland rendezvous point. This was a very dangerous undertaking, but the powder was urgently needed by the Colonial fighting forces in Virginia. Delivering the cargo to the shore by boat meant passing through the British blockade.

In order to accomplish this feat, the cargo was loaded into *The Molly's* dinghy and which was silently rowed under the cover of night to shore. All the dinghy's oars were wrapped with cloth so as to muffle the slap of the blades as they struck the water.

Upon arriving at shore, the crew unloaded the cargo at a landing at the mouth of what is now called College Creek, just down river from Jamestown. Silently, the cases of powder and boxes of shot were removed from the boat and brought ashore. By dawn an exhausted crew had successfully brought enough of the cargo to shore to replenish rebel rifles for continued action against the British.

Ship Model of an 18th Century Ship Representing
The Nicholson
The Mariners' Museum and Park, Newport News, Virginia.

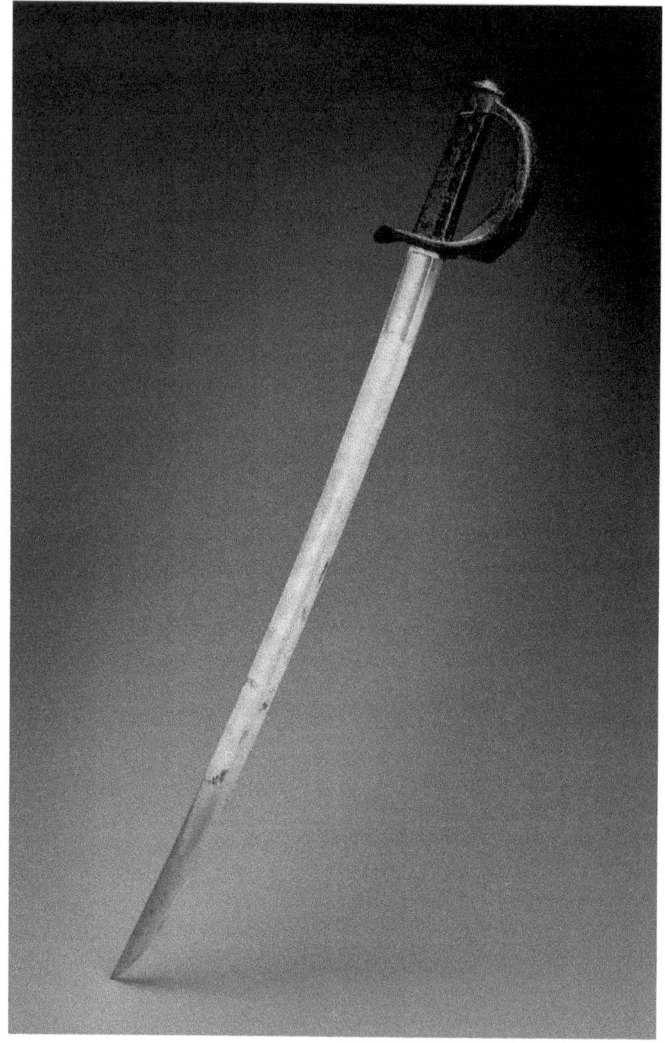

French Naval Sword representing the one given to Sinclair by Lafayette.
The Mariners' Museum and Park, Newport News, Virginia.

CHAPTER FOUR

The French (1779)

Without a decisive naval force, we can do nothing definitive. And with it, everything honorable and glorious.

– George Washington 1781

After Sinclair took command of the sloop *Molly*, *The Nicholson* remained inactive for a couple of years. Early in 1781, one of Sinclair's lieutenants named Steele took command of *The Nicholson* and then a lieutenant named Ham was the captain of the ship in September 1781. Shortly afterward *The Nicholson* was captured by the British in Virginia waters just before the decisive battle of Yorktown.

The Navies of the American Colonies, for the most part, was not very impressive and sustained great losses at the hands of the British. In June 1779, Virginia Governor Thomas Jefferson wrote:

> Our trade has never been so distressing since the time of Lord Dunmore as it is at present by a parcel of trifling privateers under countenance of two or three larger vessels who keep our little naval force from doing anything.

By the summer of 1781, the Colonial Navies desperately needed the aid of the French. Getting messages through to French naval commanders was a necessity, but British blockades made it difficult in the months before the decisive Battle of Yorktown was to take place. Lafayette needed to send a communication to

Admiral De Barras, the French Commander stationed off Rhode Island. Lafayette requested that the Virginia navy make a vessel available for carrying dispatches to De Barras. He asked for a commander experienced in running blockades and out-sailing and maneuvering the British ships. The vessel selected was the *Molly* under Captain John Sinclair.

Captain Sinclair was sent to meet General Lafayette and to receive his orders. Soon after Sinclair's arrival at Lafayette's camp, the young French General took an instant liking to Sinclair. If Captain Sinclair's demonstration of his French language speaking abilities was a ploy to impress the General, it worked. Lafayette immediately put Captain Sinclair in charge of carrying an important message to Admiral De Barras with instructions to get rid of the certain message in case of the approach of a British ship.

Captain Sinclair took the handwritten and sealed message and was off to sea. He was able to slip through the British blockade of the Hampton Roads as he had done many times and sail north up the Atlantic coast. In route, he managed to keep clear of all British vessels. *The Molly* reached her Rhode Island destination in about three days. After delivering the message to admiral De Barras, Sinclair sailed *The Molly* through the blockades and back to Virginia carrying the responding message. Sinclair was then tasked to carry De Barras' message up the James River to Lafayette's headquarters at Marvin Hill, just eight miles southeast of Richmond, Virginia.

Upon Captain Sinclair's return, Lafayette was exceedingly pleased with both captain and ship and trusted Sinclair with more missions. In recognizing Captain John Sinclair's contribution, Lafayette recommended to French

Admiral De Grasse that Sinclair be presented a French sword. The sword was not a ceremonial type, but more like an ordinary sabre. It had a plain blade but had a fairly decorative hand guard and a wooden handle. The sword was about forty-one inches in length, longer than most swords from that era. It was presented to Captain Sinclair and it remained in the Sinclair family until Sinclair's great-great grandson, Jefferson Keith Sinclair, is said to have donated it to the then called Syms-Eaton Museum in Hampton, Virginia probably in the 1950's. The sword has been missing since the 1970's.

There is one story about Captain Sinclair from 1781 that cannot be corroborated and is mostly family legend. The story relates that during the siege of Yorktown, Virginia, Captain Sinclair acted as pilot for one of the French ships in moving from the Virginia capes to the mouth of the York River. It is known that twenty-five American pilots were sent by Admiral De Grasse to pilot ships, and among those was Captain John Pasteur, Captain Sinclair's ex-first mate. The ship *Concorde* which carried these pilots, departed from Boston on June 20th bound for Havana, Cuba where the pilots were delivered on July 8th. The Spanish were friendly to the American cause and the French Navy used Havana as a base. Captain Sinclair could not have been one of these pilots because he was on a trip to Long Island in *The Molly* at this time. On his return it is possible that he might have assisted in the pilotage, but it appears unlikely. It cannot be stated categorically that this duty was not performed by Captain Sinclair as believed (or hoped) by some of his descendants, but the only support for the claim is a 250-year-old verbal account.

Captain John Sinclair loved the French and anything French. Once he even claimed to be a French citizen (which he was not). During the French Revolution in 1789, Captain Sinclair was an avid supporter of the rebel cause. Later, he let it be known that Napoleon was to become his idol and had his complete support. In gratitude, the French government presented Sinclair with a portrait of Emperor Napoleon, which he hung in a place of honor in his parlor. In 1810, upon finding out that Napoleon had divorced the Empress Josephine, he became very angry and slashed the portrait with the very sword that Lafayette had given him and flung the portrait into the fire.

In 1824 the Marquis de Lafayette made a visit to Virginia as part of the nation's fiftieth anniversary celebration. So many hundreds of Virginia citizens lined up to shake Lafayette's hand that his arm had to be propped up, probably on some sort of forked stick, so that the General would not become too fatigued.

Captain Sinclair, himself, had been deceased for years by that time, but his son, Jefferson Bonaparte Sinclair was there to greet the Marquis. They met on the old battlefield of Yorktown. When Jefferson Sinclair was introduced to him, Lafayette talked of his esteem for Captain Sinclair and reminisced about some of the duties the Captain had performed for him. Jefferson Sinclair told General Lafayette that his father always spoke highly of him also. A few years after the visit, in July 1827, Jefferson Sinclair named his newborn son, Lafayette.

Captains Sinclair's love and support of the French and everything French, would cause him problems when Britain and France went to war in 1793.

CHAPTER FIVE

After the War (1783)

Humanity has won its battle. Liberty now has a country.

– Marquis de Lafayette 1781

With the surrender of Lord Cornwallis at Yorktown, Virginia in October 1781, the American Revolutionary War was all but over. There were a few cavalry skirmishes in Georgia and South Carolina, but for the most part the fighting was over. In 1783 the Revolutionary War was concluded by a peace treaty in which the sovereignty of the United States was recognized by Britain. The treaty ended the need for privateering, and the Captain retired to the life of a gentleman farmer.

The first Federal Census, taken in Isle of Wight County, Virginia in 1782, shows John Sinclair as head of a large household consisting of his family and his nephews James and John Lattimer. James and John were the young children of Captain Sinclair's sister Margaret and her deceased husband Edward Lattimer. Edward, an officer on one of Captain Sinclair's ships, had died at sea near St. Eustacia.

By taking the young boys in, Captain Sinclair helped his sister, freeing her to rear a daughter and to remarry. As more hands on the Captain's farm were needed, the boys found ready work and were treated as brothers to John Sinclair, Jr. and Anne's four children Mary, Anne, Tom and the baby William.

With the war over, soldiers and sailors were coming home to enjoy their hard-won independence. Most were weary of the years of strife and yearned for a measure of tranquility. Among them were boyhood friends that Captain Sinclair hadn't seen since before the war. These ex-soldiers, for the most part, took up farming or trades in Isle of Wight and neighboring Surry County.

From his war related activities, Captain Sinclair had attained local fame which he found bestowed a new stature and respectability. He was asked to run for elective office but was not interested.

His retirement from sea service was at first rather pleasant for he was relieved of much of the anxiety and discomfort of that occupation. As time passed, he found full-time farming to be demanding but not always rewarding. Captain Sinclair found that he needed other interests, if only to get away for a few hours each week.

The Sinclair farm was a productive one and provided an outside income for the Sinclair family. Anne was pleased to have her husband home. Unfortunately, she was a fragile woman and had her hands full with their five children.

Captain Sinclair began to spend long hours in town where he found a mixture of business and pleasure. He missed the water but found comfort in visiting Smithfield wharves where there was much shipping activity.

Captain James Barron who was Commander of the State Boats (Virginia Navy) died in May 1787 leaving the command open for appointment. Among the applications was the one submitted by Captain John Sinclair. He apparently missed the sea life and decided he wanted this appointment.

Competition for the position was very tough with a great number of competent officers also applying. Captain Sinclair was disappointed that he did not get the appointment. It went to Richard Barron. Not getting the position had an impact on Sinclair's personality. Captain Sinclair would never again seek an office of any kind. He was not used to failure and did not like it. This rejection probably would explain the course of later events.

Living in Smithfield, Captain Sinclair was in a position to pursue his waterfront interests. He bought some trading vessels and wanted to return to seafaring in some capacity. For a while Sinclair supervised the building of necessary warehouses and wharves. Nothing pleased him more than to be consulted about ship-outfitting work.

Captain Sinclair had accumulated a great deal of money from his privateering days, but his large family was becoming expensive to support, and he had some old gambling debts to take care of. When his resources began to run low, he realized that he would have to return to sailing to raise money. Returning to the sea would be a decision the former captain would come to deeply regret.

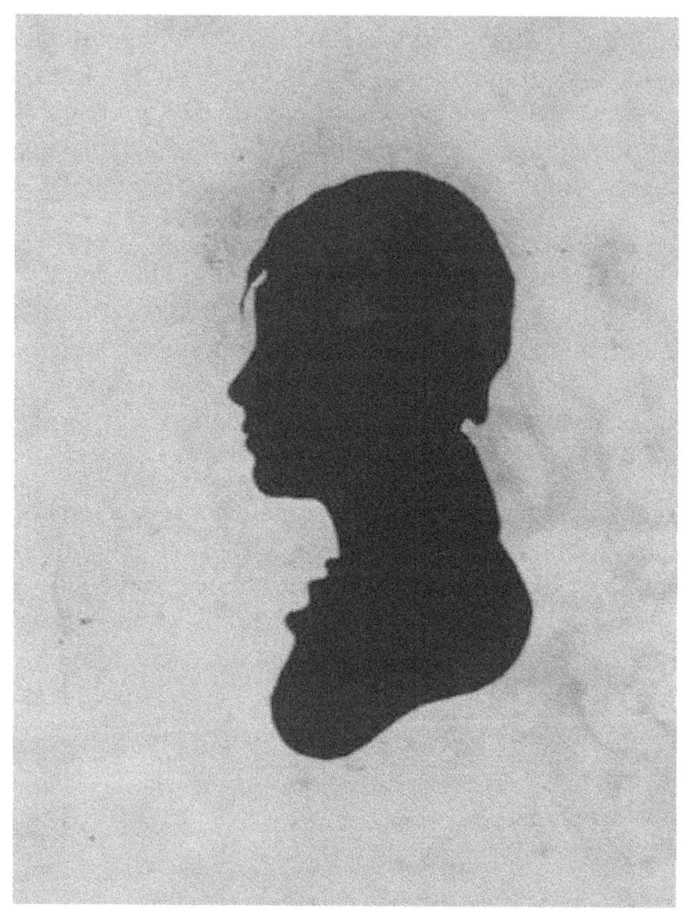

William Sinclair

Chapter Six

William (1790)

It is not flesh and blood, but heart which makes us fathers and sons.

-Friedrich von Schiller 1791

In January 1778 the Sinclairs bought their first home, on Church Street in Smithfield, Virginia (the home is still standing there today at 335 South Church St.).

The Captain's wife, Anne, was a woman of mild and affable disposition, soft spoken and docile, similar to her daughters who clearly inherited their mother's temperament. Anne and John Sinclair were truly an example of the old cliché "opposites attract."

Their first born was Margaret Sinclair in 1775, probably in Smithfield, Virginia in a house rented by Captain and Mrs. John Sinclair. Margaret tragically died in infancy. Mary John Sinclair was their second child. She was born in 1777, also probably in Smithfield. Mary was known to have a lovable personality and went by the name "Molly." Anne Elizabeth Sinclair was born into the Sinclair family in 1780. She was called "Elizabeth" and was a stubborn child. Next came Tom Sinclair, born in 1782, and then William Sinclair in 1784.

Like many fathers, Captain Sinclair hoped to have a son to follow in his footsteps, and to continue in the family tradition of men of the sea. His sons, he believed, would receive a good training under his surveillance, as well as provide companionship. The logical choice would be his eldest son Tom, but with his tendency toward seasickness Tom did not care for the sea.

Captain Sinclair's youngest son, William, was completely different. He had sea water in his veins. William was very enthusiastic about being a captain, like his father, and probably loved hearing his father tell tales of the sea.

It would have been no problem for Captain Sinclair to persuade his youngest son, six-year-old William to go on a trip with him to the West Indies in 1790. Persuading William's mother would be a different matter. Of course, there was danger in any sea going voyage and taking William would expose the young lad to potential disaster. But the nation was not at war at that time, and the Captain was used to having his way. Anne Sinclair allowed William to sail with his father. John Sinclair was looking forward to spending time with his son. They sailed out of Smithfield for the West Indies.

When the ship reached the West Indies the Captain and crew were hit by unexpected bad weather. This sort of thing could surprise any ship's captain in a time before weather reports. The Captain's only instruments were his barometer and what he could see or feel. The increase in winds and heavy cloud formations indicated that they were heading right into the middle of a storm.

Before a safe port could be reached to protect them from the heavy driving rain, the vessel struck an unseen obstruction. It probably was a rock or coral head and it broke through the hull, splintering the bottom planking, opening the small vessel to the sea. Captain Sinclair ordered that the ship be abandoned, and the exhausted crew prepared for the worst. There was little hope of swimming to shore because the storm was too fierce. There was little chance of the ship staying afloat.

Meanwhile, a frightened William clung to his father. Captain Sinclair tried desperately to swim with William on his back, but he got very tired and it was difficult for him. Other crew members offered to relieve him by taking William. Captain Sinclair would not relinquish his son even when he grew more tired. When a crew member insisted upon relieving the Captain, Sinclair steadfastly denied the proposal. The child screamed in terror as he felt his father weaken and sink deeper into the water. Finally, when it appeared the father and son were both doomed to go down together, the ship's mate forcibly took William from Captain Sinclair. William had probably panicked at being taken from his father and the ship's mate was unable to control the terrorized child. The Captain and crew were able to swim to shore, but William drowned. It is believed that the child's body was never recovered.

To say that this tragedy changed Captain John Sinclair would be a great understatement. All the joy that ever was or ever would be was drained from him. Captain Sinclair would live the rest of his life in a state of melancholia. How would he explain this tragedy to his wife, William's mother? On his return to Smithfield he discovered he would not have to.

Chapter Seven

A New Beginning (1791)

A little house well filled, a little field well tilled, and a little wife well willed, are great riches.

- Benjamin Franklin 1735

Captain Sinclair was able to "hitch" a ride home on another merchant ship. He had many friends in the maritime world, so a return voyage was probably not hard to arrange. Upon his returning to his Smithfield home, he was most likely met on the shore by one of his servants who would be there to help him dock the ship. The Captain may have also been met by his daughters Mary and Elizabeth who were only thirteen and ten years old at the time. He had terribly sad news to tell but could probably sense that his daughters had sad news to tell also.

It is not known who spoke first, but one can only imagine how the sisters may have felt upon hearing the news of their brother's drowning. Captain Sinclair may have wondered why his wife, Anne, did not greet him at the shore. The reason, as the Captain would soon find out, was that while he was at sea with William, she had also died. The only bright side of this tragedy was that she had died without knowing or experiencing the pain of hearing about William's death.

As one might imagine, the Sinclair family began to unravel a bit at this time. John Sinclair tried to patch the family back together by courting a rich widow named

Mary Ianson. As for his remaining sons, they were never again encouraged to become sailors.

On July 23, 1791 Captain Sinclair married the rich widow, Mary Mackie Ianson. Mary's husband, Andrew Ianson, had died very recently, about the same time as did Mrs. Sinclair. Mary Ianson's husband left her a large estate in Gloucester County, Virginia called "Sherwood." He also left her with three children, Archibald, Richard and Elizabeth who was only six weeks old at the time of Mary's wedding to John.

Mary is said to have been uncomfortable with the haste of Captain Sinclair's marriage proposal, but one of Mary's housekeepers talked her into marrying him. The housekeeper apparently knew Captain Sinclair well and knew that he was not the type of man to take no for an answer.

"Sherwood" was a farm that was patented in 1637 and was part of a tract known as "Robin's Neck." It was purchased by one of Mary's ancestors, Thomas Mackie, sometime after 1652. Captain Sinclair, by marrying Mary Ianson and buying out the other heirs, became the sole owner of "Sherwood." Despite owning so much property in Gloucester, the Sinclair family chose to live in Smithfield, at least for the time being.

John and Mary Sinclair had four children to add to the three that she already had plus John's three surviving children. The children of John and Mary were Caroline born in 1793, John born in 1796, Jefferson Bonaparte (named after Captain Sinclair's two most favorite people) born in 1800 and Martha born in 1803. It appears that John Sinclair was very fond of children.

Just as prospects brightened, the Sinclairs suffered another setback in the illness of The Captain's sister, Margaret. After a short illness she passed away about 1793. The loss of another family member profoundly affected Captain Sinclair, causing him to ponder his course in life. He considered retiring from active seafaring. One reason for this was his rheumatic arthritis, which got even worse at sea. Sinclair wondered if retiring as a ship captain might be prudent.

Captain Sinclair enjoyed being an independently wealthy gentleman and yet felt that he still needed another source of income. Farming did not suit him. John Sinclair decided that he would return to something he knew, the water. He began buying, repairing, building and selling ships in his own back yard in Smithfield on the Pagan River. His skills as a shipbuilder would soon be in great demand in a world seemingly constantly at war. It was a world in which citizen John Sinclair would feel at home.

Ship Model of an 18th Century Schooner Representing
The Fairplay
The Mariners' Museum and Park, Newport News, Virginia.

Chapter Eight

Back to the Sea (1793)

When men come to like a sea-life, they are not fit to live on land.

- Samuel Johnson 1824

In January 1793 France and Britain were at war again. Captain John Sinclair saw this as an opportunity for some potential privateering. There was an immediate need for privateers to sail with the French. Captain Sinclair knew that before English convoys could become well-organized, it would be possible that some good money could be made in attacking British merchant ships. But Captain Sinclair was getting older and his health made it difficult for him to actively participate in privateering.

After a substantial public debate and a great deal of private discussion over French rights and American opportunities, Captain Sinclair succeeded in arousing the interest of his wealthy ex brother-in-law, Solomon Wilson. A pact was formed between the two men for the formation of a partnership in a privateer enterprise. Wilson agreed to put up most of the money for the purchase of a vessel, a schooner named *The Fairplay,* in exchange for Captain Sinclair services as agent. Soon after the vessel's purchase, Sinclair had *The Fairplay* moved to a local shipyard where he negotiated a contract for its conversion to a war ship. Sinclair was to supervise the work himself. At the same time, he began to search for sailors and a

French proxy to whom title to the ship *Fairplay* could be passed to facilitate her transfer to French registry.

After searching for a proxy, Captain Sinclair ran into an old acquaintance, Samuel Riddick, who had only recently made an application for French citizenship to the Island of Guadeloupe for probably illegal reasons. Riddick spoke fluent French and claimed to have good connections in the West Indies. A deal was made with him to sail *The Fairplay* to Guadeloupe and arrange to transfer her to French registry. As Riddick lacked any privateering experience, Captain Sinclair wanted a different type of person to take command of The *Fairplay*.

Sinclair looked everywhere he could think of to find the right qualified man to pilot the ship. He even looked in some of the waterfront taverns and considered commanding *The Fairplay* himself.

In October 1793 Captain Sinclair finally found his man. While in Norfolk, Virginia someone referred him to William Talbot. Although inexperienced as a privateer, Talbot had captained an American merchant ship during the revolution and had experienced being attacked by British ships. William Talbot despised the British as much or more than Captain Sinclair did himself.

Captain Sinclair believed that Talbot possessed the motivation to make a good, if not excellent, privateer captain. He offered him an owner's share in the forming enterprise and the command of *The Fairplay*. William Talbot accepted.

On the 24th of November, her scheduled departure date, Captain Sinclair visited the *Fairplay* for the last time. After brief salutations the Captain gave Talbot two envelopes. The first he stated contained the *Fairplay's* sailing order and the second letter was a power of attorney to William Talbot from John Sinclair and Solomon Wilson authorizing the sale of the vessel.

On December 26, 1793, both William Talbot and Samuel Riddick applied for French citizenship and received it on December 28th. This was a necessary legality since officially the United States and Britain were not at war.

Two days later Captain Talbot sold the *Fairplay* to Samuel Riddick. Riddick filed for a name change and applied to the Governor for a commission to fit and operate his newly acquired vessel as a privateer. The *Fairplay* was now the *L'Ami de la Pointe-a-Pitre.* The *Fairplay* sailed to Guadeloupe, an island in the French West Indies to be in service to the French government.

In January 1793, Norfolk, Virginia was host to French Admiral Pierre Jean Van Stabel. Van Stabel was now in Norfolk being tasked with escorting a food convoy of ships from Norfolk to France. Admiral Van Stabel had joined the French Navy to fight for the American cause during the revolution and had served at the siege of Yorktown in 1781. He was truly a friend to America.

Captain Sinclair was among the large party on hand to welcome the arrival of the French and sought an audience with Admiral Van Stabel. The Admiral knew of Captain Sinclair, and that he was a trusted friend of the French. Sinclair was granted an audience with the admiral and upon learning that Norfolk would be the French squadron's home for a few months, he offered his services. The Admiral thanked Sinclair and told him that he might be helpful to his staff.

Before the end of the month, Captain Sinclair, with the backing of Solomon Wilson, bought a second schooner which he re-named *de la Libery* with a pilot named Edward Ballard and two deck hands. Captain Sinclair sailed the ship to the anchorage of the French naval squadron in Norfolk. He requested and received a second audience with Admiral Van Stabel and was furnished a letter which read as follows:

> In the Name of the French People. On board the Tigre, 13th of Germinal, 2nd year of the republic (April 3, 1794), &c, Peter John Van Stabel, rear admiral commanding a commission of the naval forces of the republic stationed on the coast of the United States of America. In consequences of the offer of citizen Sinclair to enter, voluntarily and from pure love of liberty, into the service of the French republic, and the engagement on his part to conduct himself altogether as a good French republican, I give him an order to take command of the schooner, de la Libery and to fulfill his commission confided to him by me (signed) Rear Admiral Van Stabel.

By the middle of March, Captain Sinclair had received news from Guadeloupe. Captain Talbot had quickly gotten his vessel and crew into fighting shape and soon proved to be the scourge of the Caribbean and in a little more than two months, the *L'Ami de la Pointe-a-Pitre*, had captured nine British merchant ships.

Sinclair decided to spend his share of the prize money by acquiring two additional vessels. John Sinclair became the founder of a Charleston, South Carolina privateering syndicate. Its two principal ships were the *L'Ami de la Pointe-a-Pitre* and the *de la Libery.*

Captain Sinclair's mood had changed after failing to be named Commodore of the Virginia Boats in 1787. His expressed bitterness from that disappointment brought about a change in his attitude toward business. Sinclair began to vigorously direct his energies to the pursuit of material wealth, something that in the past he had attached much less importance to. In working against British interests, Captain Sinclair found great satisfaction.

Admiral Van Stabel, with whom he was clearly associated with for several months in Hampton Roads, appreciated Captain Sinclair's ability and leadership as much as his courage. Captain Sinclair was ready to help the French people in any way that he was able and had a great desire to do so. President George Washington saw it differently.

President George Washington meeting with French Ambassador, Charles Genet
Harper's New Monthly Magazine

CHAPTER NINE

The American Neutrality Act (1794)

My ardent desire is...to keep the United States free from political connections with every other country.

- President George Washington 1793

The French began their own revolution in 1789 with the storming of the Bastille. France declared itself a Republic in 1792 and executed their King, Louis XVI, in 1793. The British believed that the French Revolution was a threat to monarchs everywhere and especially in Britain. They also feared that a successful revolution might give Ireland or some other British colonies ideas about revolting themselves. The loss of the American colonies was still fresh, and they did not want a repeat of that disaster. Soon the British Empire (and Spain) were at war with the French Republic.

Meanwhile, in the newly formed United States, the French Ambassador, Edmond-Charles Genet, had been actively recruiting American privateers (including John Sinclair) for attacks on Great Britain's ships. The American President George Washington, however, wanted good relations with the British now that hostilities had cooled down, and he advocated a policy of neutrality in the British-French war. In 1793, Washington proclaimed:

> Whereas it appears that a state of war exists between Austria, Prussia, Sardinia, Great Britain, and the United Netherlands, on the one part, and France on the other; and duty and interest of the United States require that they should with sincerity and good faith adopt and pursue a conduct friendly and impartial toward the belligerent Powers.

Virginia's Governor Henry Lee, Washington's friend and father of future General Robert E. Lee, was offered a commission in the French Army, but because of Washington's proclamation, was forced to turn it down.

The Continental Congress had previously made an alliance with France going back to 1778, that was instrumental in the Americans winning their independence from Britain. When President Washington had backed the "Jay Treaty" in 1794, France felt betrayed. The Jay Treaty was mostly about trade with Britain, but it led to the Neutrality Act of 1794. Many Americans, including Captain Sinclair, did not support this treaty. One reason for the Act was to create a liability for violation of the United States Constitution, which reserves to the United States Congress the power to declare war. The Neutrality Act of 1794 made it illegal for an American citizen to wage war against any country at peace with the United States (i.e. Great Britain). The Act declares in part:

> If any person shall within the territory or jurisdiction of the United States begin or set on foot or provide or prepare the means for any military expedition or enterprise ... against the territory or dominions of any foreign prince or

> state of whom the United States was at peace that person would be guilty of a misdemeanor.

The Act forbade the outfitting for war of any vessel in American waters. Many pro-French Americans were opposed to this act, and as was Captain Sinclair, who later claimed to have been ignorant of the provision of the act that would not allow the construction or outfitting of any ship for war.

Ship Model of an 18th Century Schooner Representing
The Unicorn
The Mariners' Museum and Park, Newport News, Virginia

CHAPTER TEN

The Unicorn (1794)

I wish to have no connection with any ship that does not sail fast; for I intend to go in harm's way.

– John Paul Jones 1776

By the 1790s, Captain Sinclair had a profitable shipping business sailing his vessels on trading expeditions to the West Indies and ports of the eastern seaboard. Even with the Revolutionary War being over for more than a decade, the British continued to harass American vessels, stopping and searching them and occasionally impressing some of the crew into British service. This only increased Sinclair's hatred of everything British, if that were even possible.

By 1794, it became common knowledge in Smithfield that a three-mast barkentine type ship called *The Unicorn* was being out-fitted for war and repaired at Sinclair's wharf on the Pagan River, just behind his own home. The rumor around Smithfield was that its intended use was as a privateer ship to assist the French in their continuing fight with the British. Most of the people of Smithfield were sympathetic with the French cause, and because of their fondness for the Captain, turned a blind eye and a deaf ear toward his questionable activities.

The Unicorn was a Baltimore built ship bought by Captain Sinclair in 1793. She was about 65 feet long and had sharp lines for fast sailing. Captain Sinclair may have purchased the ship as an investment, hoping to refit her and sell her at a profit.

On July 6, 1794, John Hamilton of the British Counsel in nearby Norfolk, learned that T*he Unicorn* was being refitted along the Pagan River by Captain Sinclair. Hamilton wrote to Governor Henry Lee of Virginia on that very day:

> I am authentically informed that John Sinclair and others of Smithfield, as now fitting out a large ship as a privateer to carry twenty guns, and that a Capt. Doharty…now in this place and Portsmouth [Virginia], are enlisting and recruiting men for said ship.
>
> This is contrary to an act of Congress passed last session, you will no doubt take such steps as appears to you proper to put a stop to the equipment of the said ship contrary to the laws of neutrality, and to the above act of Congress made for such purposes.

Counsel John Hamilton was quite aware that Captain Sinclair was known to be a French sympathizer.

Governor Lee reported this to U.S. Attorney General Alexander Campbell who, on July 11, wrote to the Governor directing him to investigate:

> It having been represented to your Excellency by the British Consul at Norfolk, that a Mr. Sinclair and some other persons at Smithfield, are fitting out a ship to act as a privateer in the present war of Europe; I shall consider it as my duty if this shall appear to be true, to prosecute on the part of the United States for the forfeiture and penalties which have been incurred by this violation of their laws.

Meanwhile, William Lindsay, a tax collector at nearby Norfolk, Virginia, was also interested in what was going on with Sinclair's new ship. He asked his representative at Smithfield, Copeland Parker, the Surveyor of the Port of Smithfield to investigate.

This was a difficult task for Parker, who had a personal relationship with Captain Sinclair and also wished to marry the Captain's daughter, Elizabeth. Parker probably felt that it was his patriotic duty as well as his job to fairly and professionally investigate Sinclair and was most likely not personal. In his report to William Lindsay, Parker stated that *The Unicorn* was being fitted out as an armed vessel and that her upper deck had been cut down to support cannon.

Parker sent his report, dated July 8, to William Lindsay, Collector of Customs at Norfolk, about what he had found out:

> The ship appears to be about 65 feet keel, 24 Beam, 9 feet hold, was built during the late war in Maryland, is sharp built, and must sail fast from appearance; her upper Deck has been cut down. She now appears to be fitting for an armed vessel, having a slight waist run-up, with eleven portholes of a side. She is under the direction of Mr. John Sinclair, a native of this country, who has expatriated himself by law and calls himself a citizen of France [Sinclair was never a French citizen]. He has many men employed upon the ship, and from appearances she may be ready to sail in three weeks. A number of guns are laying by her, which is intended for her, and from every appearance she is designed for a Cruising vessel. What may be Mr. Sinclair's intentions, I do not know, but it is generally said she is to go to sea well-armed and well manned with citizens of the United States. It is thought by some that she has been commissioned by Admiral Vanstable (sic), by others that she is to go to a French port, and there obtain a commission to act against the enemies of the French Republic.

William Lindsay forwarded this report to Governor Lee on July 16. Lindsay also added:

> I have received information from Mr. Parker...that a vessel has arrived there from Baltimore with 300 four-pound balls, and a considerable quantity of powder and grape shot for the further equipment of the said ship.

Governor Lee sent his own man, Lt. Col. Samuel Butler, to investigate the rumors. Lt. Col. Butler consulted the Colonel Commandant of Isle of Wight Co., James Wills of Smithfield.

Meanwhile, by the time Lt. Col. Samuel Butler questioned Captain Sinclair a week later, the Captain had been tipped off. He had removed all war material from *The Unicorn* and locked it in his storehouse. Captain Sinclair told Lt. Col. Butler that *The Unicorn* was not intended for use as a privateer. He said that he had sold one-half interest in her and it was the part-owner's wish that the deck had been cut down (for cannon use). Lt. Col. Butler had also been misled by Colonel Jim Wills of the Isle of Wight County, Virginia militia, who said that he had personally found out that the rumor that *The Unicorn* was being fitted out as a privateer was unfounded.

On July 15,1794 Samuel Butler wrote the Governor as follows:

> Col. Wells told me there had been such a report, and in consequence thereof he had endeavored to obtain every possible information concerning it, but that he had not been able to establish the fact, nor did he believe it was the intention of Mr. Sinclair or anyone concerned in the ship, to fit her out for the above purpose. After making the fullest inquiry of every dis-interested person from whom I could expect to receive

> the smallest information and having strictly examined the ship. I waited on Mr. Sinclair and interrogated him respecting the matter. He solemnly declared to me that the ship was not intended for a privateer."

When Governor Lee received these conflicting reports about *The Unicorn*, he started another investigation. This one led by U.S. Marshal D.M. Randolph and U.S. Army officer Major G. K. Taylor. They arrived on Saturday, July 19, 1794 in Smithfield and first approached Copeland Parker who retold his original report and added that a shipment of munitions had also come in and was probably in Captain Sinclair's storehouse.

The two men next went to Colonel Wells [of the local militia] to gain his cooperation in their investigation. They had orders to gather evidence, seize *The Unicorn* and make whatever arrests were necessary. Col. Wells, being a friend of Captain Sinclair, only pretended to cooperate when he was asked to bring his militia.

Nevertheless, Major G. K. Taylor of Norfolk, and Marshal D. M. Randolph were sent to Smithfield to seize the ship. Later, they sent hurried dispatches to the Governor stating that they had been insulted and threatened with violence by the people of the town. They also went on to say that the local militia under Colonel Wells and Major George Benn were reluctant to assist in seizing and holding the vessel. Mr. Randolph wrote to the Governor in his letter dated July 19, 1794.

> I have received formal warning from Sinclair, to wit, that if 500 men attempt to search his house and his life shall be forfeit, he will put the first man to death. He [Sinclair]...came to my side of the ship for this purpose, attended by a Capt. Malcomb, who was armed with a sword and pistol. The first was wrestled

> from him whilst it was exhibited over the vessel's side and wounded in a very trifling degree one of my men (by accident I believe). The pistol he walked off with, swearing that whoever should take that from him, should receive two balls through the headfirst.

Major Taylor added a note:

> We are informed from sources too respectable to afford room for doubt, that in a house contiguous, a number of cannons, musket and balls, and a considerable quantity of powder are deposited. The house, Capt. Sinclair has informed me, he will lose his life defending.

Taylor and Randolph did not undertake to search the house under these circumstances, evidently believing Captain Sinclair was a man not to be trifled with, but requested further directions in the matter, and armed reinforcements. Twenty-five soldiers and three officers were then sent from Norfolk to Smithfield aboard a revenue cutter. However, Governor Lee, considering the force insufficient to the resistance, dispatched Brig. Gen. John Marshall (later Chief Justice of the U.S. Supreme Court) with two companies of the Prince George [County] Infantry (a considerable body of militia), to march against Smithfield. General John Marshall, clad in the full uniform of a brigadier general of the Virginia Militia, rode on a black steed through the town at the head of a body of cavalry, with flags flying, established a military formation on Church Street right in front of Captain Sinclair's home.

Before the arrival of General Marshall and his militia, Captain Sinclair enjoyed the support of the people of Smithfield. It was thought by many that the town's people would revolt and drive off any soldiers that would attempt to invade Sinclair's home or try to take his ship. This changed. The people seemed to be fascinated by this display of military force and pageantry. The crowd around the troops seemed to get larger and larger by the minute. Soon, some of the people stepped forward and offered their full support for whatever the soldiers intended to do. The supporters of Captain Sinclair slowly, one by one, left the crowd and went home.

General John Marshall, finding that even the thought of resistance was abandoned upon his arrival, began a peaceable search of the Sinclair home and the adjacent storehouses. He reported to Governor Lee on July 23th that:

> Thirteen pieces of cannon, with some ball, grape shot, and powder was found. There were pieces lying on the shore… The Marshall [Randolph] received personal insult [from Sinclair], and seems not to have been free from personal danger… Captain Sinclair declares that he never designed to violate the law; that the arms found in the house were not intended for the *Unicorn*, but were purchased for a gentleman to the Southward; that the balls will not fit the [*Unicorn's*]cannons, and that though she was originally designed as privateer, the intention was changed so soon as the act of Congress prohibiting vessels to be armed in our ports was known;

Finally, Marshal Randolph, with the Prince George Infantry, boarded *The Unicorn.* He told Sinclair that he was seizing the ship and that he was under arrest, Sinclair was soon released on his own recognizance.

Major Taylor wrote of this incident to Governor Lee on August 4th:

> At the head of the band, I advanced armed with a pair of pistols and followed by the Colonel [Wills] unarmed to the relief of the Marshal [Randolph], who

> had according to agreement, precisely at six o'clock, taken possession of the Ship, arrested Captain Sinclair, and ordered him and the workmen from on board her....[the workmen] threatening to cast Marshal overboard if Captain Sinclair would only give the word.

General John Marshall also wrote to the Governor on July 28th:

> There were, however, strong circumstances which might readily induce an opinion that violence was contemplated. The night after the *Unicorn* was seized, persons were heard for a considerable time loading firearms in the house of Captain Sinclaire (sic). The drawing of iron ramrods and ramming down the charge were distinctly heard....It is with great regret I mention an accident which befell one of the Prince George Infantry...The company from Prince George was on board, and was ordered neither to go on shore, or to permit any person from the shore to come on board the vessel. A militia man who had stolen out, attempted to return, and on being hailed by the sentinel attempted to rush by him without an answer. It was so extremely dark, that person could not be distinguished, and the sentinel at the same time pushed with his bayonet and attempted to fire. The rain which had fallen fortunately prevented the discharge of the musket, but a dangerous wound was received from the bayonet.

Fortunately, cooler heads prevailed, and no one was hurt except for the wounding of Capt. Malcomb and the soldier from the Prince George Infantry. President George Washington and Secretary of War Henry Knox were made aware of these events by Governor Lee.

Meantime, Captain Sinclair found out that U.S. Marshal Randolph would soon move the *Unicorn* to Bermuda Hundred for the internment. Sinclair managed to arrange for a captain, known to him, to pilot the ship and to have some of his own men among the crew. Then he went to Norfolk to further his plans for recapturing the *Unicorn.*

By Wednesday, June 23rd, all the supplies from Captain Sinclair's storehouse were loaded on *the Unicorn.* Some of General Marshall and Captain Sinclair's own men were to remain onboard for the trip to Bermuda Hundred and the cutter was to act as an escort. Captain Sinclair went to Norfolk locating a vessel and rounding up a pilot and a crew there. His plan was to capture *the Unicorn* and sail her to Guadeloupe in the West Indies. Perhaps he had a buyer there.

When Friday morning came, Captain Sinclair had not yet been able to locate any gunpowder for his attack. *The Unicorn* sailed as planned. It was Sunday, June 27th, before Captain Sinclair located the gunpowder he needed. The plan was discovered which made it hard to obtain gunpower. It was fortunate for Sinclair that his plan had failed had he been successful, Captain Sinclair would have found himself in far more trouble with the law. Captain Sinclair's next battle would be in court.

6-pound Naval Cannon C. 1754 representing a Cannon
from *the Unicorn*
The Mariners' Museum and Park, Newport News, Virginia

The Courthouse
Williamsburg, Virginia

CHAPTER ELEVEN

The Trial (1794)

It is more important that innocence be protected than it is that guilt be punished.

– John Adams 1770

Had Captain Sinclair been tried a mere twenty years before, he would have been tried in British America and not in the newly formed United States. His trial would have been much different and not as fair. Because of the freedom people like Captain Sinclair had fought for, he would be tried by a jury of his peers and would be assumed innocent until proven guilty.

Two separate court actions were started. The first was a libel of *The Unicorn* under Section 3 of the U.S. Act of Neutrality of 1794 which provided for confiscation of any vessel outfitted contrary to the Act. The second proceeding, listed against Captain John Sinclair, was a criminal action under the Act of Neutrality that held violators chargeable with a high misdemeanor. A conviction for Captain Sinclair could mean a fine and imprisonment.

Tradition says that General Marshall and Captain Sinclair were old friends who had served together in the early days of the Revolution. In spite of this, the basis for the indictment of the vessel and Captain Sinclair was that Marshall had reported that "the obvious design of *The Unicorn* as a privateer and the contents of the Sinclair storehouse produced "strong circumstances" which might readily induce an opinion that violence was contemplated."

The hearings were held at the Courthouse in Williamsburg, Virginia in early September 1794 and the trial was set for early November of that same year. The Courthouse was built in 1770 and still stands today on Duke of Gloucester Street.

The Judge was to be George Tucker a resident of Williamsburg. On November 6 at District Court in Williamsburg, Captain Sinclair was asked a series of questions. He stated in court that *The Unicorn* had been purchased by him in 1793. At the time of its seizure, *The Unicorn* was equipped for commerce and not war. His plan was to carry flour as cargo. No guns, ammunition or any war-like materials had been purchased for her.

Captain Sinclair solemnly declared that *The Unicorn* was not intended as a privateer, that though modified for such service, his intention for her proposed use was changed as soon as the Act of Neutrality "prohibiting the arming of vessels in our parts" was known to him. Sinclair also stated that the arms found in the house were not intended for *The Unicorn* but were purchased for an unnamed gentleman, and that the cannon balls found in his stowage would not fit the cannons he also had in stowage and therefore could not be used for any kind of warfare or piracy.

On November 6, 1794 a jury of his peers acquitted Captain Sinclair. His acquittal was partly due to the defense showing the cannon balls that Sinclair had in stowage would not fit the cannons and together could not be used in war. The true reason for Sinclair's quick acquittal was probably the fact that he was a Revolutionary

War hero and very well-liked and respected in his community.

Nevertheless, on November 25, 1794, a grand jury indicted Captain Sinclair, returning a true bill upon the charge of having fitted out a privateer. The Government was unable to block the dismissal by the Court of the charge against him.

The final court record stated:

> This day came as well the attorney for the United States as the defendant by his attorney who being heard: It is considered by the Court that the Indictment be quashed and that the defendant recover against the United States his costs by him about his defense in this behalf expended.

The Unicorn was returned to Captain Sinclair. He used the ship for commerce as he had said was his intent all along. The Government attempted to retry the case, but it was finally dismissed on June 6, 1797. The Court ruled Sinclair could recover the cost of his defense against the United States. His next trial would be a family one, and one that he could not win.

Anne Elizabeth Sinclair

CHAPTER TWELVE

Elizabeth (1796)

To have known love, how bitter a thing it is.

– Algernon Charles Swinburne 1866

Captain Sinclair understood his sons. That could not be said of his daughters. From his two marriages, he had five daughters. He was father to three by his wife Anne, including Margaret (who died young), Mary and Elizabeth and two by his second wife, Mary, including Caroline and Martha. John Sinclair's girls perplexed him and even more so as they got older.

Anne Elizabeth (called Elizabeth), was named for her mother and was said to be much like her mother in temperament and personality. Captain Sinclair's affection and endearment for her was greatly increased and deepened with the loss of his first wife.

As Elizabeth became a young woman, she began to receive the attention of a neighbor, a slightly older gentleman from a good Smithfield, Virginia family. His name was Copeland Parker, a surveyor of customs for the port of Smithfield. The couple fell in love, however, because of their age difference (she was 12 years younger) and the fact that his family were not considered wealthy, the Captain was not too keen on the idea of this match.

When Copeland Parker asked Captain Sinclair for permission to marry his daughter, the Captain reluctantly gave his approval. Meanwhile, the romance continued to grow. Sinclair was beginning to get used to the idea of a marriage until the onset of *The Unicorn* incident in July of 1794.

As the Smithfield representative of the tax collector at Norfolk, Copeland Parker, was obligated, if not duty-bound, to investigate *The Unicorn* and to find out if it was being outfitted as a privateer vessel.

When Captain Sinclair discovered that it was Copeland Parker who was the one investigating him, he was furious and bitter. He forbade his daughter from ever sharing Parker's company again and barred Copeland Parker from his house and property forever. Captain Sinclair would not compromise or listen to reason. He was completely inflexible on this matter.

The forbidding of Copeland and Elizabeth being together only resulted in a stronger bond between them and more distance between Elizabeth and her father. For several months, Elizabeth and Copeland met in secret but only when Captain Sinclair was out of town.

Through the year 1795 Captain Sinclair remained, hopeful of moving the family to a new home in Gloucester County, Virginia mostly just to keep Elizabeth away from Copeland. Captain Sinclair thought that by taking Elizabeth to Gloucester she might catch the eye of another young man and who would turn her attention to someone more suited.

When the Captain was out of town or at sea, he instructed his wife, Mary, to do everything that she could do to keep Elizabeth and Copeland apart and to prevent their meetings by any means necessary. Mary did all that she could do to follow her husband's directions but was not very successful.

Meanwhile, Copeland Parker, fully aware of the hatred that Captain Sinclair felt for him, mustered the courage to plead his case to the Captain on behalf of Elizabeth and himself. Captain Sinclair was shocked and surprised at Parker's actions, but his reaction was still predictable. He replied that "there was no avenue or access nor power on earth" that could change his mind.

On Sunday January 25th, 1796, Captain Sinclair set sail from Smithfield for the West Indies on a routine trading trip. The next day, and just barely out of the Chesapeake Bay, he had an uneasy feeling that something was wrong at home. He then did something that he had never done before. He turned his ship around and returned to Smithfield.

Upon his arrival, he quickly learned why the misgivings that had prompted his unprecedented return were valid. He was told that Elizabeth and Copeland had eloped to North Carolina shortly after his departure. Elizabeth was now the enemy. John Sinclair disowned Elizabeth as his daughter. He never spoke to her again.

In four days, the newlyweds returned to Copeland Parker's residence on Church Street (lot 56) where they intended on making a home, actually only a few yards from the Sinclair home. They had hoped for forgiveness or a family reconciliation, but it was not to be. Many of their friends visited and wished them well, but they were completely ignored by the Sinclair family. Captain Sinclair instructed all his remaining family members not to ever speak to or about Elizabeth or Copeland or to any of their children they may have in the future. It was as if the Parker family did not exist.

Five weeks after Elizabeth's marriage, the Sinclairs sold their home on Church Street. Captain Sinclair started building a new house at a site overlooking the Severn River. A house where Elizabeth and family were never to cross the threshold. The chosen site was in fact close to the location of the outpost Captain Sinclair had used as a base for privateering. The house was to be called "Lands' End." The house is a two-story, three-bay, steeply pitched gambrel-roofed brick building. The house remains there to this day and is on the National Register of Historic Places.

As the months and years went by, there was no change in Captain Sinclair's hostility toward his daughter. Sinclair was even unmoved by the birth of his own grandson, a boy named Nicholas, born in July 1797. Neither was he moved by the birth of a second child, born in 1798, a girl named Anne Sinclair Parker. Elizabeth and Copeland Parker were to have six children, two boys and four girls. John Sinclair had nothing to do with any of them.

The Parkers moved to Norfolk in January of 1800 and were by all accounts a happy family. However, none of the children made any attempts to contact their grandfather as they and he grew older.

In February 1807, Elizabeth died suddenly in childbirth, although the infant (their sixth and a girl) survived. Copeland wrote in his diary:

> Although her father during this long period has remained implacable in his resentment toward, her and carried out his cruel threat to never forgive her for marrying against his wishes, yet I hope his animosity is now buried with her early grave.

Parker's wish was not fulfilled. Not only did Captain Sinclair never reconcile his feelings with his grandchildren, but in his 1815 will he posthumously disinherited Elizabeth (who had been dead for about eight years. He also left his innocent grandchildren by Elizabeth, one dollar to be divided between all of them.

Land's End c. 1930

CHAPTER THIRTEEN

U.S. War with the French (1798)

And ye shall hear of wars and rumours of wars

– The Gospel According to St. Matthew (KJV)

In the aftermath of the French revolution, the French monarchy was abolished in 1792, and a French republic was born. Consequently, the United States refused to continue repaying its huge debt it owed to France from loans funding the American War for Independence. The U.S. claiming debt void because it was owned to an entity no longer in existence. France was also angry that the United States was actively trading with Britain, with whom France was at war. In response, France authorized privateers to conduct attacks on American shipping, seizing numerous merchant ships and ultimately leading to an undeclared war between the two countries in 1798.

In this American quasi or undeclared war with France, the Congress authorized President John Adams to issue Letters of Marque to private armed vessels. With this act French vessels taken as prizes became liable to condemnation for the benefit of the privateers.

Captain Sinclair would have no part of it. He believed that Great Britain was the real enemy and his fondness for the French had not changed. He seemed to take no interest in the so-called war and rarely even spoke of it. If Captain Sinclair had been offered a Letter of Marque to be a privateer, he certainly would have refused it. Sinclair spent his days working his farm and enjoying the pleasure of life as a country gentleman.

By late 1800, the United States Navy, the British Royal Navy and the French Navy had reduced the activity of the French privateers and warships. The Convention of 1800, signed by Napoleon, ended the United States – France Quasi-war. The agreement between the two nations ensured that the United States would remain neutral in the wars of France against Britain. The United States was also free of debt to the French Republic.

Captain Sinclair would soon be involved in a new kind of war with his family, in which he refused to be neutral.

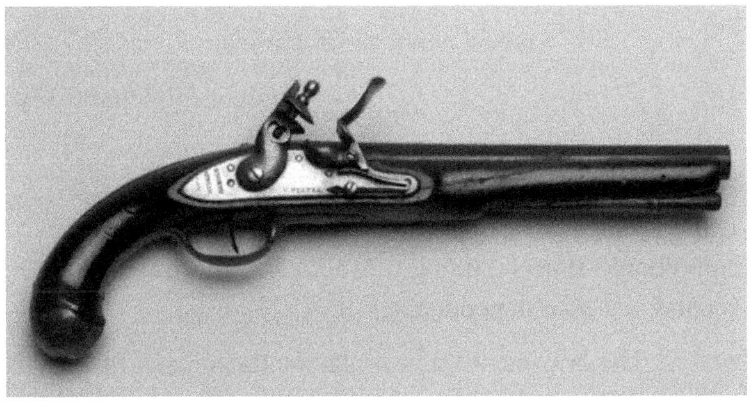

1808 Flintlock Navy Pistol representing one used
by Captain Sinclair
The Mariners' Museum and Park, Newport News, Virginia

CHAPTER FOURTEEN

The Second War of American Independence (1812)

Everywhere I turned to execute my plan, the [British] Royal Navy got in the way.

- Napoleon Bonaparte 1805

What is often called "The War of 1812" in the United States is seen in Britain as a minor theater of the Napoleonic Wars. To many Americans, the war was the second war of independence.

The origins of this war can be dated back to 1807 when the British introduced a series of trade restrictions which negatively affected American trade with France, whom Britain was fighting in the Napoleonic Wars. The still young United States contested these restrictions as illegal under international law. Britain felt that the United States presented a threat to British maritime supremacy. The American merchant marine had nearly doubled between 1802 and 1810, making it by far the largest neutral fleet. Britain was its largest trading partner, receiving eighty percent of American cotton and fifty percent of other American exports, and the British public and press were resentful of the growing mercantile and commercial competition. The United States' view was that Britain's restrictions violated its right to trade with others.

During the Napoleonic Wars, the British Royal Navy expanded to 176 war ships and 600 ships overall, requiring 140,000 sailors to man them. The British Royal Navy could not get enough manpower from just volunteers, so it turned to impressment, or forcing men to serve in their navy.

The British Navy considered any American citizen liable for impressment if he was born British. This, of course, angered the American public, however, the US Navy also forcibly recruited British sailors.

In 1812, when the Americans declared war on Great Britain, Captain Sinclair was fifty-seven years old and not in the best of health. Although taking up arms against the British seemed appealing to him, he was not particularly inclined to be directly involved in any privateering activities. Along with arthritis and other ailments, his eyesight had become poor over the years.

Captain Sinclair was requested by the United States government to help locate, survey and designate suitable craft for commandeering. Ships were needed to repel or discourage British landings along the Virginia coastline.

It was said that during this war, Captain Sinclair carved a wooden figure of a British soldier and painted it with a "red coat" royal dress uniform. This wooden figure was about 10 inches long. It was suspended by a string around its neck similar to a hangman's noose and was hung from a pully on the ceiling. The string was attached to a door, so that when the door was opened the suspended Brit would fall and rise when the door was closed. Captain Sinclair's hatred of the British had not changed. The feeling may have been mutual. Captain Sinclair owned at least two commissioned privateer ships in the War although he did not personally command any of these ships. There were many sea battles and much privateering in the waters near Lands' End. Captain Sinclair may have been a personal target of British attacks.

At one point in the war a British ship was near "Lands' End" with the obvious intention of sending a force ashore to raid for provisions. Captain Sinclair rounded up all the arms in the house and headed with all available hands, including his two sons, John and Jefferson, to the anticipated landing. Jefferson Sinclair was only twelve years old and was too young to handle the big guns and could not steady them. One of the servants fixed a forked stick in the ground allowing young Jefferson to rest his gun muzzle in the crotch. All of the guns were aimed at the boatload of British sailors rowing toward the shore. As the boat came within range of the guns, the Sinclairs opened fire from the shore. Gunfire was returned by the sailors in the British boat. Together, Captain Sinclair and his sons put out enough of a volley that the boat turned back. The landing was entirely averted and after some firing from the longer-range guns on the ship, the British withdrew.

By 1814, both the Americans and the British had achieved their main goals or were tired of the war. They both sent delegations to Ghent, Belgium and negotiations were concluded on December 24, 1814. They agreed that the war would end in a stalemate after agreeing to terms.

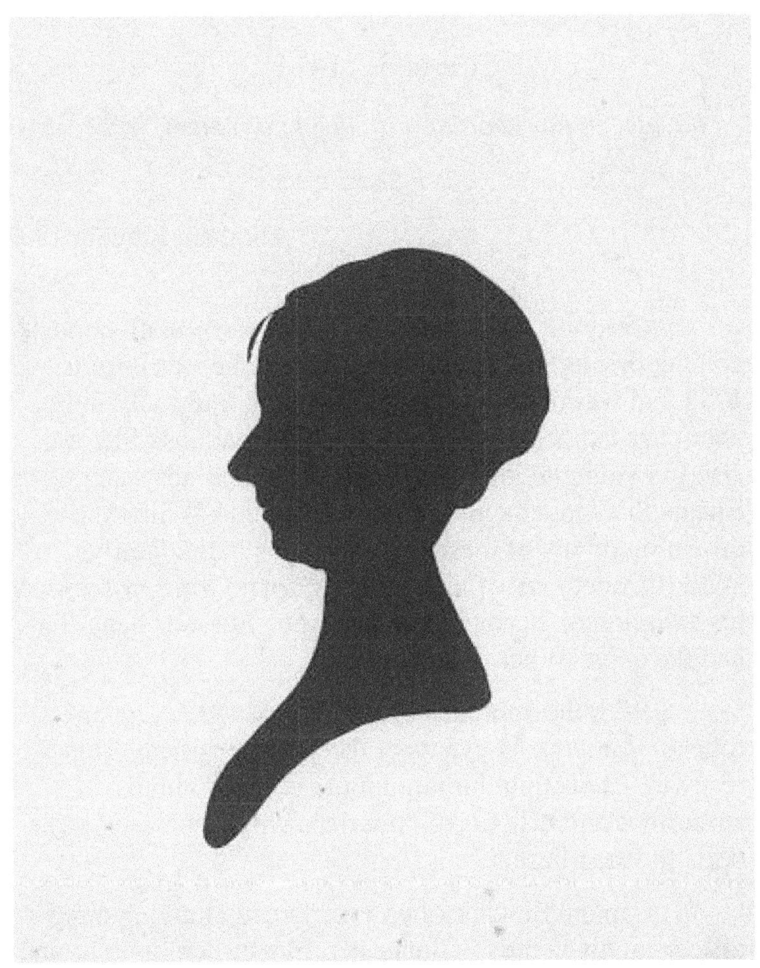

Caroline Sinclair

Chapter Fifteen

Caroline (1816)

I have been too familiar with disappointments to be very much chagrined.

– Abraham Lincoln 1832

Caroline was Captain John Sinclair's sixth child and the first by his second wife Mary. She was born in 1793 and was of course far too young to know anything about her father's pirate conspiracy allegations. She was also too young to know anything about her half-sister Elizabeth's elopement or about her brother William's drowning or any of these early tensions in the family. With Elizabeth out of the picture, Captain Sinclair focused his attention on his daughter Caroline. She was beautiful and the apple of her father's eye.

With the approach of the War of 1812, Captain Sinclair's interest in events of the sea intensified. This renewed interest put him into more contact with naval authorities and officers of American ships who used local ports for their base.

Captain Sinclair often entertained eligible young officers at his home in Gloucester, mostly sea captains and Navy personnel. One such young officer was naval Lieutenant Jesse Elliot. Lieutenant Elliot had dinner with the Sinclairs and took a liking to eighteen-year-old Caroline and she felt the same. Captain Sinclair thought very highly of Lieutenant Elliot, so when the Lieutenant and Caroline became engaged, Captain Sinclair was delighted. To him, it seemed like a perfect match.

The engagement happened quickly, but the wedding had to wait. Lieutenant Elliot was scheduled to go out to sea for a few months. The coming United States war with Britain made heavy demands on U.S. ships and its sailors.

Caroline and Lieutenant Elliot agreed that on the day of his return they would be married. The making of all the plans and arrangements made for great excitement in the Sinclair family. The wedding was to take place at "Lands' End."

On the appointed day, Lieutenant Elliot, arrived at "Lands' End" by water as was the plan. The night before the ship's crew gave him what today would be called a bachelor party. Gifts were given and there was much drinking and celebration with the ship's cannons firing. The plan was that his ship would sail close to "Lands' End" and Lieutenant Elliot, dressed in his finest Navy dress uniform, would take a small boat to the shore and meet Caroline. The wedding ceremony was to be outside near the "Lands' End" dock. After the ceremony, Lieutenant Elliot and his bride were to row the boat back to the ship where they would have their honeymoon.

Lieutenant Elliot borrowed a small boat from the ship and began to row toward the dock at "Lands' End." As he got closer to the dock that morning, he was puzzled about why he saw no one on the shore at "Lands' End." He was sure he was in the correct place on the shore. As he got closer, he could see only one man standing on the dock. He instantly became overwhelmed with anxiety. "What had gone wrong," he must have asked himself.

As his boat approached the dock, Lieutenant Elliot was approached by the man, a servant of the Sinclairs. He was carrying a message, a letter to Elliot from Caroline, which he handed to Elliot. The short note stated that she had a change of heart. The planned ceremony, it added, had been cancelled. The note said only that she had met someone else. With the lack of technology in that day, there was no way for Caroline to communicate her change of heart to Lieutenant Elliot any sooner. Both Lieutenant Elliot and Captain Sinclair were broken hearted.

An embittered Lieutenant Elliot abruptly rowed back to his ship with his men still cheering thinking that Caroline was with him.

Upon his return to his ship, Lieutenant Elliot was greeted with a booming cannon salute. All of the naval vessels anchored as well as the shore batteries joined in under the mistaken belief that Elliot was returning with his bride. This salute lasted about twenty minutes and only caused more embarrassment for the lieutenant. It was as if the celebration was there to mock him.

Lieutenant Elliot moved on and soon married Frances Vaughn and had a very successful naval career. Captain Sinclair never got over it.

Caroline married Cary Selden Jones in 1816. Caroline and Cary Jones' wedding was in the Sinclair home, but Captain Sinclair refused to attend or give the bride away. Sinclair said," I have given her to one man, sir, I shall not give her to another."

During the wedding ceremony, Captain Sinclair stayed upstairs in his bedroom in bed although he was not sick. After the ceremony Caroline and Cary Jones, as man and wife, entered Captain Sinclair's bedroom, knelt by his bed and begged him for his forgiveness. Sinclair only looked away.

In spite of being very disappointed with Caroline, Captain Sinclair let the couple live in a cottage on his property. As for Captain Sinclair, he was ageing fast. He was growing tired of fighting the British and everyone else. He died at his home at Land's End in 1820 at the age of sixty-five years. Caroline and Cary inherited Sinclair's farm.

Sinclair Memorial Plaque

EPILOGUE (1820)

Much like his hero and idol Napoleon, John Sinclair was a tyrant who hated tyrants. He died a bitter man in 1820 and was buried at his "Lands' End" estate. In 1971, a memorial anchor and plaque were placed at the "Lands' End" estate by Claude O. Lanciano, Jr. who owned Lands' End at that time. The plaque reads:

This memorial marks the last anchorage of the American patriot, privateer, and alleged pirate…

Captain John Sinclair

1755-1820,

In is not known what became of *The Molly* after the war. Presumably she had sunk around 1794. *The Nicholson* was sold to Lieutenant Steele. In 1781, she was captured by the British. As for the infamous ship *The Unicorn*, all that is known is that it was sold to a Frenchman by the name of Peter Marshall. Marshall changed the name of his ship to *The Bouillon* and mounted her with twenty-four cannons. Sometime later *The Bouillon* was reported to have attacked a Danish ship off the coast of Virginia in an act of piracy.

Robert Munford Sinclair (1838 – 1907)
Captain John Sinclair's Grandson

Georgiana Wray Sinclair (1842 – 1904)
Captain John Sinclair's Granddaughter

Maude Roberta Sinclair (1859 – 1932)
Captain John Sinclair's Great-granddaughter

APPENDIX

Sinclair Descendants (1820)

There are only two lasting bequests we can give our children -

one is roots, and the other, wings.

-Hodding S. Carter 1942

Captain John Sinclair's oldest surviving daughter, Mary Jones Sinclair, moved to Mississippi as a young adult. For many years "Aunt Polly" as she was known, corresponded with the Virginian branch of the Sinclair family, but seems to have just disappeared during the American Civil War.

Captain Sinclair's disinherited daughter, Anne Elizabeth Sinclair, had six children with her husband Copeland Parker. Two of her daughters married into the Jones and Allmand families and have many descendants living in Virginia and elsewhere. Elizabeth died young and was buried in her mother's family plot.

Elizabeth's husband, Copeland Parker, was never able to patch things up with his father-in-law the Captain. He died in 1830. A poem on his gravestone reads:

Traveler stop! Reflect on what I was,
On what I am, on what you soon must be.
I once was young, I once was vain-
I once was dust, am dust again!

Tom Sinclair, the Captain's oldest son, was a disappointment to his father for reasons that are not clearly known. Tom moved to Mississippi with his sister Mary and is said to have married a woman from that state. Tom and his wife had a daughter they named Margaret. After Tom had separated from his wife, he moved back to Gloucester with his daughter Margaret in 1813. His father, the Captain, gave him a tract of his plantation. It consisted of 61 acres of marsh on the Ware River. His father also built a home for him. Tom, although only 31, was then a sick man. He died in 1815, five years before his father's death. Captain Sinclair included his granddaughter, Margaret, in his will. She fared a little better than her cousins by their Aunt Elizabeth. She was willed one dollar to keep all for herself.

Sinclair's disappointing daughter, Caroline, who married Cary Selden Jones, had eleven children. After her father's death, she and her family moved from the Bay Cottage on the Lands' End property into the main house. After her children had grown, some of them moved into their father's family home in Hampton, Virginia. Their house burned down during the American Civil War's "burning of Hampton" in 1862. The family took refuge in Richmond where many of Caroline's grandchildren died in an epidemic.

John Sinclair, Jr. (named for his father the Captain) was the Captain's next oldest son. He became a gentleman farmer and planter. John married first Margaret Ann Munford in 1820. After Margaret's death in 1837 he married Lucy Baytop. John had a total of eleven children.

One of John, Jr's. daughters was Mary Munford Sinclair (1822 - 1902) who married Thomas Booth Taliaferro (1818-1879). Mary was a great storyteller of her grandfather's exploits. She is also the great grandmother of actress Glenn Close.

One of John, Jr's. sons was named Robert Munford Sinclair. He married his stepmother's sister Rowena Baytop in 1855, and during the time of the American Civil War, he and his wife and children lived with his in-laws, the Baytops. One of the young slaves at the Baytop farm was T.C. Walker who grew up to be a famous lawyer and civil rights leader.

When the Civil War broke out, Robert Sinclair became a member of the 5th Virginia Cavalry. It was very dangerous for him to visit home, since Union troops often raided farms in the county. Once, when Robert was home on leave from the war, he was almost captured by the Union Cavalry.

Years later his daughter, Maude Sinclair, wrote of an incident that had taken place when she was about four or five years old:

> Whenever the Yankees came, someone would give the alarm and things were looked after. The first time I saw the Yankees come riding in the yard, I was at first pleased. They had pretty blue uniforms all trimmed in gold, and brass buttons and braid and such pretty horses and outfits that would glisten in the sun. Grandma [Lucy Taliaferro Catlett Baytop] would go to the door and talk with the officer while the rest of the men would wait for his orders. I remember the officer called to his men and they followed him to the smoke house and ordered Grandmother to unlock it and took all of the bacon that was in there and then took their sabers and fished out the beef from a barrel until all was gone. They would strap the dripping wet beef behind their saddles and rode off with it. Grandma told them she had a large family to feed but they would only laugh as if it was a joke. I would see tears in her eyes but didn't realize what was going on to cause them. Another time they came and ordered their canteens to be filled with all of the milk she had, so they went to the dairy and the canteens were all filled until the last drop was gone. But the cows were left. They always asked for the silver and searched the house from

> top to bottom. I remember once my Father [Robert Sinclair] was at home from the war when the Yankees came. He did not have time to get out before they came in the house. In my mother's room there was a closet with a little door cut in the ceiling which led back some distance and it was very dark in there; so Papa as we called him, took some food and his pistol which hung by his side and went in that little dark hole. I saw him do it and one of those Yankees asked me if any men were in the house and I said that my papa was. He wanted to know where and I pointed to the closet. The soldier looked in the closet and opened the trap door only to see my papa's pistol pointing in his face. The Yankee backed away telling his superior officer that there was no one there. What a narrow escape my father had.

In 1880 Maude Sinclair married Alexander Taliaferro Wiatt, a man nineteen years her senior. Maude and Alexander Wiatt are the great-grandparents of this author, Thomas Taliaferro Wiatt.

John, Jr., also had a son named William Baytop Sinclair (1862-1955) who married Annie Bell (1865-1939). Annie wrote down many of the family stories about Captain John Sinclair that she had heard from relatives. These writings proved to be an invaluable source of information for this book.

Captain John Sinclair's next son was Jefferson Bonaparte Sinclair. He married Georgiana Wray, had seven children and for a time lived in Hampton, Virginia until their home burned down. The family then moved back to Gloucester County, Virginia.

Since Jefferson was born in 1800, he was too old to participate in the American Civil War. On one occasion, during a raid of Gloucester by Federal troops, Jefferson was stood against an oak tree in his yard. The troops then threatened to shoot him if he didn't tell where the family money and silver were hidden. In a loud voice that would have made his father proud, he told the troops, "You can shoot me, but you cannot scare me." The Federal troops let him go.

Some of Jefferson and Georgiana's Sinclair descendants settled in Hampton near what was later to be called the Sinclair (traffic) Circle near where the International House of Pancakes (IHOP) restaurant is today on Mercury Blvd. After the Civil War burning of Hampton of 1862, many of the Hampton citizens took refuge on the Sinclair farm. One of Jefferson and Georgiana's many descendants was Hunter Booker Andrews the one-time Senate Majority leader of the Virginia State Senate.

Georgiana Wray (Mrs. Jefferson Sinclair 1806-1877) deserves much of the credit for what is now known about Captain John Sinclair's life. She related stories to her granddaughter, Indiana Lowry (Mrs. James Jefferson Sinclair 1864-1962) who in turn passed them to her daughters, especially Georgiana Wray Sinclair (1889-1952).

Captain Sinclair's last child was named Martha Mary John Sinclair and she was born in 1803. She was called Mary and was a bit of a tomboy. She married Alexander Jones who was also the brother of her sister Caroline's husband Cary Selden Jones. Captain Sinclair was not pleased that another Jones was courting his daughter. He stated that if Mary married Alexander Jones, she would be cut out of his will "without a shilling." Fortunately for Mary, she waited until after the old captain's death before she wed. Mary and Alexander had one child named Elvira in 1833. Elvira married Dr.

George Cooper and the couple moved to Baltimore, Maryland.

Captain John Sinclair's descendants now number in the thousands. Their surnames read like an old telephone book of Eastern Virginia. They include Allmand and Andrews, Beavers and Booth, Collier and Curtis, Field and Floyd, Jackson and Jones, Parker and Phillips, Lankes and Lilley, Rhodes and Robins, Selden and Smith, Tabb and Taliaferro, Wiatt and Wray, and so many more.

Tom Wiatt visiting the National Civil War Naval Museum in Columbus, Georgia. He is standing next to the uniform & sword of his second cousin 4 times removed Catesby Jones, the Commander of the Ironclad Virginia.

ABOUT THE AUTHOR

Thomas T. Wiatt is the great-great-great-great-grandson of Captain John Sinclair. Tom was born in Savannah, Georgia and lives in Newport News, Virginia. He is a graduate of Virginia Tech in Blacksburg, Virginia and Thomas Nelson Community College in Hampton, Virginia. Tom is a retired Engineer from Newport News Shipbuilding and is presently an Engineering Consultant at Gibbs & Cox, Marine Solutions. He is also a volunteer at the Mariners' Museum and Park in Newport News. Other than history and writing, his passions include music and world travel. He is also the author of the books *Rev. William E. Wiatt* and *Captain Sally.*

BIBLIOGRAPHY

Allmand, Barbara J., *Three Virginia Families – Allmand, Parker, and Sinclair: including a collection of 19th century letters and other writing*. Copyright 1995, B.J. Allmand, Overland Park KS.

Beveridge, Albert J., *The Life of John Marshall*. Copyright 1919 Houghton Mifflin Company New York, NY.

Dashiell, Segar Cofer, Article in Newport News, Virginia *The Daily Press,* December 31, 1961.

Evans, Cerinda W., *Some Notes on Shipbuilding and Shipping in Colonial Virginia.* Copyright 1957, The Mariners' Museum, Newport News, Virginia.

Jones Family Papers, Swem Library, College of William and Mary

Henderson, John W.S., *Caithness Family History*. David Douglas Publisher, 1884

Konstam, Angus., *Privateers & Pirates 1730 – 1830.*, Copyright 2001, Osprey Publishing Ltd. Oxford, UK.

Lanciano, Jr., Claude O., *Legends of Lands' End.* Copyright 1971, Lands' End Books.

Lanciano, Jr., Claude O., *Capt. John Sinclair of Virginia.* Copyright 1973, Lands' End Books.

Rouse, Parke, Jr., *John Sinclair and the Virginia Navy*, The Ironworker 39: 2-11.

Sanchez-Saavedra, E.M., *A Guide to Virginia Military Organizations in the American Revolution, 1774-1787.* Copyright 1978, Virginia State Library, Richmond, VA.

Selden, Jefferson Sinclair, Jr., *The Sinclair Family of Virginia – Descendants of Henry Sinclair Born in Aberdeen Scotland.* Copyright 1964, Jefferson Sinclair Selden, Jr.

Sinclair, Caroline B., *The Kidnapped Child*, Copyright 1983, McClure Printing Company, Inc., Verona, VA.

Sinclair, Caroline Baytop and Sinclair, Margaret Munford, *Biographical notes of Captain John Sinclair, privateersman, ship owner and Captain in the Virginia Navy of the Revolution*. Unpublished. 1955.

Toll, Ian W. *Six Frigates: The Epic History of the Founding of the U.S, Navy*. New York: W.W. Norton. C. 2006

Tormey, James, *The Virginia Navy in the Revolution – Hampton's Commodore James Barron and his fleet.* Copywrite 2016, The History Press, Charleston, SC.

Tucker, George. Article in Norfolk, Virginia, *The Virginian-Pilot,* September 25, 1994.

Virginia Gazette 1751 – 1780. Williamsburg, Virginia.

www.ingramcontent.com/pod-product-compliance
Ingram Content Group UK Ltd.
Pitfield, Milton Keynes, MK11 3LW, UK
UKHW020240250726
13967UKWH00001B/469